My Perfect Brown Boy

By Britni Nicole

**For my son Dexter,
I love you always and forever.**

My perfect Brown boy
was born in the spring

4

5

My perfect Brown boy is
as happy as can be!

My Perfect
Brown Boy is always
smiling up at me.

And My Perfect Brown
Boy is so handsome
can't you see?

My Perfect Brown Boy
has curly, curly hair,
that twist and turns all
through the air.

My Perfect
Brown Boy has the
softest brown skin, it
glows in the sun and
radiates from deep
within

My Perfect
Brown Boy was made
perfectly for me.

My Perfect
Brown Boy loves cars,
trains, and planes

19

And My Perfect Brown Boy loves music. He sings and dances and grooves to every beat.

My Perfect Brown Boy loves to build, draw, and create. His imagination is quite breath taking and has no limitations.

My Perfect Brown Boy is so very smart. There isn't anything this perfect Brown Boy can't do.

24

My perfect Brown Boy is so strong, brave, and courageous.

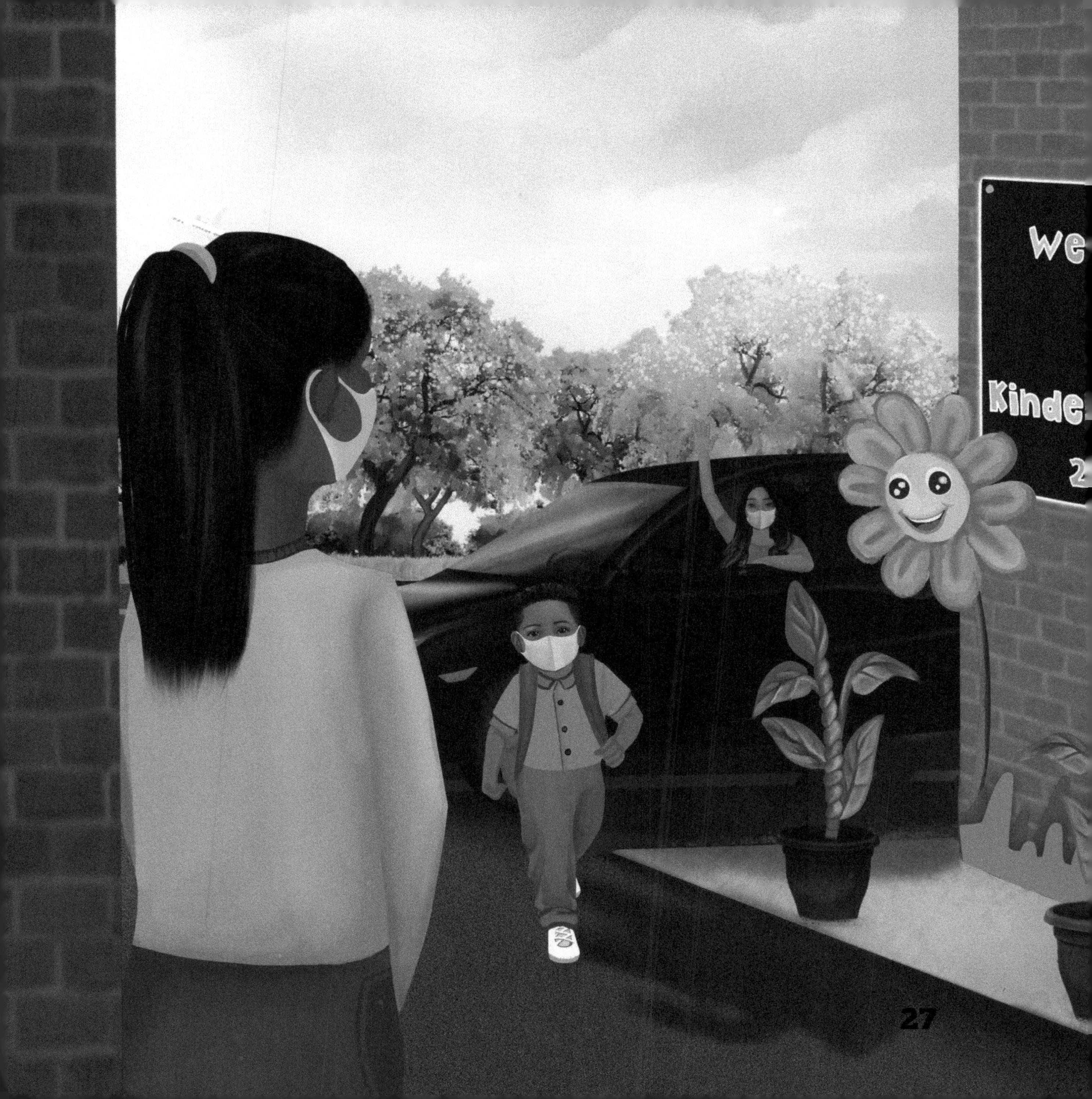

We
Kinde
2

And My Perfect Brown Boy will stand up for those around him. For he has never feared; he has faith built within.

29

But My Perfect Brown Boy is also a sweetheart. He loves to cuddle and snuggle, and his kisses and hugs are quite phenomenal.

My Perfect Brown Boy loves to chuckle, His hee hee and ha ha's are from sunup to sundown. He laughs and laughs with every tickle of his tummy.

My Perfect
Brown Boy will always
be protected, loved, and
covered.

For My Perfect Brown Boy is so remarkable. He's the best part of me and my love for him is untouchable.

36

First day in Kindergarten

My Beautiful brown boy

37

I love my
perfect Brown Boy!

My Perfect Brown Boy name is Dexter.

What is your name Perfect Brown Boy?

CPSIA information can be obtained
at www.ICGtesting.com
Printed in the USA
JSHW011956020622
26592JS00006B/6

9 780578 347110